WHEN CHRISTMAS CAME TO BETHLEHEM

FLEMING H. REVELL COMPANY

WHEN CHRISTMAS

CAME TO

BETHLEHEM

CHARLES L. ALLEN
CHARLES L. WALLIS

Acknowledgment is gratefully made for permission to reprint lines:

From "Journey of the Magi" from COLLECTED POEMS OF T. S. ELIOT, copyright, 1936, by Harcourt, Brace & World, Inc., and reprinted with their permission.

From "The Death of the Hired Man" from COMPLETE POEMS OF ROBERT FROST. Copyright 1930, 1939, by Holt, Rinehart and Winston, Inc. Reprinted by permission of Holt, Rinehart and Winston, Inc.

From *J. B.* by Archibald MacLeish, 1958. Reprinted by permission of Houghton Mifflin Company.

From "Credo" from COLLECTED POEMS OF EDWIN ARLINGTON ROBINSON, copyright 1929, The Macmillan Company. Used by permission.

From "The Wisest of the Wise" from *Christmas Chimes in Rhyme* by Ralph W. Seager, © 1962 by The Judson Press; reprinted by permission of the author.

Preface

Some of our Christmas customs are as spiritually valuable as a second-hand coffin. They are broken cisterns which no longer hold the sweet waters of eternal life. They may seem tinsel-bright, but they lack depth.

A metropolitan store posted a sign reading, "We have no Christmas greeting cards left, only religious ones."

In these pages we turn from external to internal meanings. We look, insofar as we are able, within, not without. We seek not the incidental, but rather the fundamental promises of Christ's coming.

Christmas nowadays is big business, but for Christians it is unfinished business. Into our hurly-burly, topsy-turvy world, which rests uneasily fifteen minutes from an atomic holocaust, comes once again the promise of "on earth peace, good will toward men."

A youngster, counting the striking of a clock, became fearful when the strokes exceeded twelve. "Mother," he exclaimed, "it's later than it's ever been before!" But the day is not so far spent that we may not once more read knowingly the words of Joseph Fort Newton: "The race will never know salvation unless it is love-lifted and star-led."

When Christmas came to Bethlehem God expressed Himself in Personality to personalities. Bethlehem is a story of throbbing hearts and wistful faces, not digits in a mechanical census computer, and of individuals, not statistics in an annual report. This book is about the human beings and the Divine Being whom God placed within the nativity story. We feel that they are our invisible companions. "There is no speech nor language, where their voice is not heard" (PSALM 19:3). Through them may we come to understand better that our insignificant lives are precious to God.

Contents

Contents

WHEN CHRISTMAS CAME TO BETHLEHEM

1

Christmas and Ordinary People

IS ANYTHING as common and at times more monotonous than the ordinary days of our lives? One day after another, and every one so similar. Exciting things happen to other people, but we are consigned to life's back pages. Eagerly we anticipate tomorrow, but our best-laid plans fizzle out like Roman candles. Hopefully we mix the ingredients of spunk, stamina and courage, but always some malicious Herod comes along and throws sand in the soup. We bravely read Shakespeare's noble words:

There's a divinity that shapes our ends,
Rough-hew them how we will.

But that's not for us. Heroically we gird for battle,

but alas, we cannot move in Saul's armor. Our fate is that of Robert Frost's hired man:

Nothing to look backward to with pride,
And nothing to look forward to with hope.

Then comes Christmas. Christmas is our day. Christmas is for ordinary folks. Now once again we hear the beat of a distant drummer. Now we hitch all of our hopes to a shining star.

That is how it was when Christmas first came to Bethlehem. Even the setting of the nativity was commonplace. A sequestered town astride a limestone ridge, where once Jacob gently laid to rest his beloved Rachel, where Boaz claimed Ruth as his bride, and where the prophet Samuel anointed the head of the shepherd lad, David—but now, overshadowed by the splendors of Jerusalem, Bethlehem, "little among the thousands of Judah" (MICAH 5:2), is a spent candle.

Two weary travelers enter the village on a night that can scarcely be distinguished from a thousand other nights. Bureaucracy must have more tax moneys! And a Child is born. A Child. Not Athena sprung fully grown and fully armored from the head of Zeus. Not a resplendent king descending in a flaming chariot from the heavens. Only a birth, the most common of human experiences. This is how God comes.

One would have expected the burst of a meteor, a brilliant sun at midnight, a burning bush, a pillar and a cloud, a parting of the waters. But none of these things happens. A Child is born at the hour of twelve, so pious legend tells us, to a mother of humble origin. We should have thought God would have chosen dawn when the heavens are aglow with the variegated colors of the rising sun, or twilight when the hand of day reaches high to pull down the purple curtains of the night. How strange are the ways of God!

Yet the very ordinariness of that first Christmas pleads knowingly and persuasively to common people. Christmas came to little Bethlehem that we might know that no place is unknown to God; at the stroke of twelve to remind us that there is no moment of the day or night when He is absent from us; to young Mary to convince us that all life is dear to Him; and in a Child that we may sense all of life is in His hands. Christmas is His monogram, stenciled on our hearts, recalling to us year by year that "no more is God a Stranger."

Christmas is person-centered. Christmas affirms that human lives—"even the least of these," like Mary, the shepherds, a Baby—are the least expendable treasures in the whole universe. W. H. Auden in *For the Time Being* says that on this day

Everything became a You and nothing was an It.

The God of Bethlehem is not concerned with principles, abstractions and theories. He loves only people. He is the Good Shepherd who searches in love for even the least worthy and most neglected of the children of men.

Will Durant in *The Story of Philosophy* writes of another kind of deity:

"Aristotle's God never does anything. He has no desires, no will, no purpose. He is activity so pure that he never acts. He is absolutely perfect. Therefore He cannot desire anything. . . . His sole employment is the contemplation of himself. Poor Aristotelian God. He is a do-nothing King. The King reigns but does not rule."

Not so the God and Father of our Lord Jesus Christ. Dr. J. B. Phillips' translation of John's Canticle of the Incarnation reads:

"At the beginning God expressed Himself. That Personal Expression was with God and was God, and He existed with God from the beginning. All creation took place through him, and none took place without Him. In Him appeared Life and this

Life was the Light of mankind. The Light still shines in the darkness, and the darkness has never put it out (John 1:1-5)."

God's supreme revelation of Himself is through Personality—the Personality of Christ—so that we ordinary mortals may know and understand Him. And in the years of His ministry among men Jesus cast His lot within the vortex of human experience, linked Himself to our common human destiny, and died on a cross for such persons as you and me. Wrote John Robert Seeley in *Ecce Homo,* "He set the first and greatest example of a life wholly governed and guided by the passion of humanity."

Do you wonder that Christmas is especially precious to ordinary people? Or that on this day, more so than on any other, we think of giving, not getting, and of what we can do for others, not what they can do for us?

The nephew of Ebenezer Scrooge expresses the genuine Christmas spirit in response to his uncle's assertion that Christmas is humbug:

"I am sure I have always thought of Christmas time, when it has come round—apart from the veneration due to its sacred name and origin, if anything belonging to it can be apart from that— as a good time; a kind, forgiving, charitable, pleasant time: the only time I know of, in the long calendar of the year, when men and women seem by one consent to open their shut-up hearts freely, and to think of people below them as if they really were fellow-passengers to the grave, and not another race of creatures bound on other journeys. And therefore, uncle, though it has never put a scrap of gold or silver in my pocket, I believe that it *has* done me good, and *will* do me good; and I say, God bless it!"

Nearly twenty centuries have come and gone since Christ's coming to Bethlehem. But even now He comes.

Where meek souls will receive Him, still
The dear Christ enters in.

Read prayerfully these words from the pen of Dr. Albert Schweitzer:

"He comes to us as one unknown, without a name, as of old by the lakeside he came to those men who knew him not. He speaks to us the same words, 'Follow thou me,' and sets us to the tasks which he has to fulfill for our time. He commands. And to those who obey, whether they be wise or simple, he will reveal himself in the toils, the conflicts, the suffering which they shall pass through in his fellowship, and as an ineffable mystery, they shall learn in their own experience who he is."

Christmas has staked a claim on our ordinary lives, making them vessels of adoration and instruments of praise. Always this has been true. To the last syllable of recorded time this will remain true.

2

She Cradled Him in Love

WHERE WITHIN all history and literature may we find a more wonderful story than the nativity of Christ? This old, old story lives and glows with a new vitality each time we turn to its pages. Defying the ravages of time, the familiar words never become wearisome.

During twenty centuries men of creative genius—musicians, poets, artists, and persons possessing disciplined skills—have come under the spell of the gospel message and have dedicated such treasures of talent as no other day may claim.

Although craftsmen have adorned and embellished Christmas, human ingenuity could never have originated this story. John Sutherland Bonnell rightly exclaims, "Only God could have dreamed the Christmas story."

Why do we cling, after so many centuries, so

tenaciously to the simple words recorded by the evangelists? Why does the worldwide Christian fellowship, numbering more than 900 million persons and representing every stature and degree of our common humanity, find Bethlehem to be the fountainhead of joy, inspiration and redemption?

Bethlehem surely means many things to many people, and no genuine meaning is without significance. But towering over all, Christmas is a story of divine and human love. Christmas is a festival of love which has a magnetlike tug on our hearts. A compelling, compassionate and all-encompassing love explains the attractiveness of this day. Without love, there could never have been a first Christmas. Apart from the love we bring and the love we offer and receive, Christmas would be as dreary as an all-day drizzle.

Central to the meaning of Christmas is the love of our heavenly Father as interpreted and translated in the birth of His Son. This great, undeserving and self-giving love of God to men is at the heart of the testimony of the early Christians.

For God so loved the world, that he gave his only begotten Son, that whosoever believeth in him should not perish, but have everlasting life (JOHN 3:16).

. . . God sent his only begotten Son into
the world, that we might live through him.
Herein is love, not that we loved God, but
that he loved us, and sent his Son to be the
propitiation for our sins (I JOHN 4:9-10).

Behold, what manner of love the Father
hath bestowed upon us, that we should be
called the sons of God. . . (I JOHN 3:1).

Nor height, nor depth, nor any other
creature, shall be able to separate us from
the love of God, which is in Christ Jesus
our Lord (ROMANS 8:39).

Can our minds comprehend the mystery and
marvel of it all? How shall we explain such divine
prodigality? "And all they that heard it wondered
at those things which were told them by the shepherds" (LUKE 2:18). And so do we. We can say only
that God loves us as He does because He is God, and
we can shout with joy that He cared enough to
send His greatest blessing!

There is so much about us that speaks in a differ-
ent, and an indifferent, tongue. The accent of the
universe is one of dispassionate impartiality. Not so
with God. His accent is one of passionate partiality
—even for us.

God loves us because He hopes thereby to claim us

for Himself, to save us from the stupidity of tread-mill living and from the foolishness and folly of our sinfulness, and to raise us from our split-level living to the height and nobility of heroic and victorious spiritual achievement.

And what can we do about it?

> Love so amazing, so divine,
> Demands my soul, my life, my all.

We may respond with all we have got to give. When God woos us with such loving compassion, can we turn from Him?

Christmas is also a love story because of Joseph, who rose above his questionings and doubts and gave himself heart and soul to Mary whom God had chosen as a worthy vessel by which His love might be made manifest. We could have understood if Joseph had turned from Mary, but he did not. His faith transcended his misgivings. He enfolded her helplessness in his strong arms after God's messenger had said, "Joseph, thou son of David, fear not to take unto thee Mary thy wife: for that which is conceived in her is of the Holy Ghost" (MATTHEW 1:20).

Joseph ministered to Mary's needs as they made their tiresome pilgrimage from Nazareth to Bethlehem for the enrollment ordered by Caesar Augustus. He sought reposeful quarters for her, and when her hour had come, he was at her side. For her safety he led her and the Child to a distant land beyond the reach of Herod's wrath. Later he guided them back to his home in the hills where he devotedly provided a home which, though perhaps unostentatious, knew such comfort and protection as only self-effacing love offers. The love of God is mirrored in the heart of the rugged carpenter of Nazareth.

Christmas, furthermore, is a love story because Mary cradled the Child in the arms of a tender and dedicated love. The life of Mary is an exquisite tapestry woven with those golden threads which we find in all loving and sacrificial motherhood.

The Lord of highest heaven, whose creativity is proclaimed by the spacious firmament, whose power is flaunted in orbiting spheres, and whose sovereignty no man can gainsay, unveiled His love in a Babe reared with loving care and concern within a home. God thereby made holy the hearth, and He hallowed the family altar. Since that distant day the life within the family circle has been sacramental.

Christmas is a family day. "Home for Christmas" are the words on the lips of earth's prodigal children. This is a day for joyous family reunions, a day when, perhaps more so than on any other day, young and old rejoice in each other's good company. This is also the day when we remember especially the vanished voices and the empty chairs at the Christmas table.

When Christmas came to Bethlehem, love came too. And Jesus, who was cradled in the arms of Mary's love, has ever since blessed all families and tightened the bonds of Christian love. And He has stretched our hearts to enclose all men within the circumference of our love, for He teaches us that God has "got the whole world in His hands."

The elemental lesson in the school of Christ is that we love Him because He first loved us, and that we love others, both the lovable and the unlovable, in His name.

Don't let this Christmas pass by without realizing the challenges and compulsions on the frontiers of Christian love. The old and familiar words of Kate Douglas Wiggin are worthy of remembrance:

> *My heart is open wide to-night*
> *To stranger, kith or kin.*
> *I would not bar a single door*
> *Where Love might enter in.*

3

The Forgotten Man
at Bethlehem

A WORRIED mother phoned the church office on the afternoon before the annual Christmas party of the Sunday school to say that her small son, who was to play the role of Joseph in the Christmas play, had a cold and had gone to bed on doctor's orders. "It is too late now to get another Joseph," the teacher replied. "We'll just have to write him out of the script." And they did, and very few of those who watched the play that night realized that the cast was incomplete.

Joseph of Nazareth is the most neglected person in the Christmas story. Who would think of Christmas without singing angels, bright-eyed shepherds, sedate and regal Wise Men, a pompous and blustering Herod, or even a frantic and nervous innkeeper?

We couldn't have Christmas without them! But Joseph—well, we often write him out of the script.

Maybe our ignoring of Joseph is something most fathers can understand. "Good old dad" nods resignedly when his children clamor for new clothes. He tags along when mother goes to school to check on Johnny's grades. He stays in the car while the family does the shopping. He waits in the next room as the children share their little confidences with mother. He twiddles his thumbs helplessly in the hospital lobby when his children are being delivered, and he feels somehow neglected and out of place at his daughter's wedding party.

Perhaps we excuse our forgetfulness of Joseph in sermons, song, art and verse by saying that, after all, Joseph was a pretty common man who added very little to the excitement and spectacle of the gospel story.

Joseph's hands were calloused by his toil in a little carpentry shop in Nazareth. He never wrote his memoirs. He didn't utter imperishable words—nowhere in the Bible is a single word of his quoted. He looked with awe upon the wisdom of those who had mastered ancient lore, and he profoundly respected those who spoke with an erudite authority which was incomprehensible to one having his limited schooling.

The word "ordinary" describes Joseph. And who ever gets excited over such persons? Who—except, perhaps, God? God, who is no respecter of persons, looks benevolently upon all men. To him no man is mean or common. The word "ordinary" is not to be found in the vocabulary of Deity.

If the landscape of Joseph's world was horizontally cramped and confining, his skyscape knew no limitations, for his soul was ever sensitive to and also responsive to things spiritual. God was no stranger to his heart. He knew the diction and syntax of eternity. When God spoke, Joseph understood and obeyed. His mind was infiltrated with a glory of a higher sphere.

There is a man like Joseph in every church. He is faithful, dependable, helpful and considerate. He makes no splash and draws no attention to himself, but he turns off the lights when the others have left, he locks the door, and he takes home a heart heavy with the burdens of others. And "of such is the kingdom of heaven" (MATTHEW 19:14)!

Men like Joseph are the salt of the earth and the yeast in the dough. They are the key logs in the jam of human relationships. H. G. Wells may well have had such men in mind when he wrote, "There dwell eternal gallantries and eternal generosities within the heart of man." And God knows how to detect strength in meekness and to employ obscure saints in His Kingdom.

"What kind of a preacher do you have?" a man asked an acquaintance. "He is a lighter of lamps in a dark world," was the reply. This is the kind of person Joseph was, and the lamps he lighted still shine brightly. We would do well to remember this forgotten man at Bethlehem. He is a person we should know more about.

If an epitaph were to be chosen to identify the final resting place of Joseph, these words would be particularly appropriate:

A JUST MAN

And these are the very words Matthew uses to describe Joseph.

Little information about him may be gleaned from the gospels. The occasional references to him are like pieces of a crossword puzzle which must be patiently arranged if a portrait is to emerge. When, however, this has been accomplished, we have before us an individual who is worthy of our praise and veneration.

In the gospels we read that Joseph, after he had become engaged to Mary, discovered that she was anticipating the birth of her first child. Before he was told the truth regarding her situation, he considered the possibility of severing his betrothal in such a way that she might not be unduly disgraced or shamed. Then God revealed to this godly man His eternal purpose which would be made evident in the birth of Mary's son.

Joseph then gladly became her husband, attended her at the hour of Christ's birth, arranged for the safety of mother and Child during their flight into Egypt, and later provided both a home and companionship for the Lad.

By heritage, Joseph was in the royal lineage of King David. By vocation, he was a carpenter. Because no direct reference is made concerning him after Jesus' twelfth year, we may presume that he died when Jesus was still young.

Matthew speaks of Joseph as being "a just man." These words may be translated as "a righteous man." "Righteousness" in those days was a stronger word than it is in our common usage. "Righteousness" meant uprightness before God. Joseph lived to the best of his ability in a right relationship with God.

Something of the righteousness of Joseph may be suggested to us by Jesus' own teaching regarding man's duty and responsibility to God. Through the ministries of Jesus the words and disciplines of Joseph have permeated the centuries. Who can fully measure the good which issues from the life of a just and righteous person?

When Christmas came to Bethlehem, Jospeh of Nazareth found a purpose for his life within the greater purposes of God. And so may we. When we link our little lives to God, we become uncommonly essential in the economy of eternity.

4

Christmas
at Their Doorstep

JOSEPH AND MARY journeyed eighty-five miles along dusty roads from Nazareth to David's City for the Roman enrollment. The Wise Men, following caravan routes which were ancient even in Solomon's day, traveled untold distances from their far-flung oriental kingdoms. But the shepherds of Bethlehem bowed reverently at the manger of the Christ Child who was born within the range of their voices. Christmas at their doorstep! How very fortunate they were! And on a night when they least expected it, they were singled out for an everlasting glory in music and art and poetry.

These hearty men of Bethlehem were tending their flocks when an angel of the Lord appeared unto them. Nothing like that had ever happened to them before. In fact, nothing much ever happened to disturb the monotony of their lives. Occasionally, of course, a rustle among the flocks made it evident that an intruder, perhaps a wolf, lurked nearby. But when the danger passed, the shepherds piped softly a tune on their reed instruments and the sheep became calm once more. The shepherds then sang a folk song their fathers had taught them, or passed the never-ending hours of their nightly vigil swapping grandfather stories and munching on olives, bread and dried figs.

But this night was unlike all of the others. The sky became radiant with a light not of this world. Read again the words of the time-cherished story as found in LUKE 2:9-14:

> And, lo, the angel of the Lord came upon them, and the glory of the Lord shone round about them: and they were sore afraid. And the angel said unto them, Fear not: for, behold, I bring you good tidings of great joy, which shall be to all people. For unto you is born this day in the city of David a Saviour, which is Christ the Lord. . . . And suddenly there was with the angel a multitude of the heavenly host praising God, and saying, Glory to God in the highest, and on earth peace, good will toward men.

Glory be! Such a great honor for so small a town. Such a tremendous message for the ears of common men. But why not? Were not these very likely the same fields where Israel's hero, David, had once tended flocks and sung of green pastures, still waters, and divine guidance through the valley? God had returned to His favorite people, the shepherd folk from whom Abraham, Moses, Amos, and a host of other spiritual giants had come. To these common men who had for generations bred spotless and unblemished lambs for temple sacrifices came the proclamation of the Good Shepherd and of the Lamb of God which taketh away the sins of the world.

Naturally the shepherds were fearful when the shadows were pierced with light and a celestial choir, the first Christmas carolers, made the heavens quiver with a message of God's love. What a magnificent memory would be forever enshrined within the memories of those shepherd lads!

But their fears did not long persist. At the angel's bidding, they went "with haste" to see for themselves "this thing which is come to pass, which the Lord hath made known . . ." (LUKE 2:15-16). The words "with haste" are meaningful. The shepherds did not hesitate, nor quibble over questions and doubts, nor prolong their decision until a more convenient season. One of the splendid things about those shepherds, who were wise in a lore not gleaned from books, was that, when God spoke, they did not dillydally but rather responded with a wholesome spontaneity which puts to shame our misgivings, qualifications, reservations and equivocations when God calls to us.

"Let us now go . . . and see." Well, they may well have reasoned, we have nothing to lose and possibly everything to gain. Were the good tidings too good to be true? Nay, too good not to be true. And they found Him whom they sought!

There are arresting and challenging aspects in the experience of those shepherds. First, the glorious news came when they were engaged in their common chores. A shepherd's work was not exciting.

In summer's heat, and winter's cold,
He fed his flock, and penn'd the fold.

Probably the Judean shepherds would long before have escaped from their tedious labors if they could have, but they couldn't. And often we can't either, however beckoning may be all that lies beyond the horizon. We have our work to do and responsibilities we cannot shrug off. Contented or not with our lot in life, we have no alternative other than to do the task at hand, which, if we are not diligent, will never get done.

How often God comes when we least expect Him and when we plod on with never a hope to see a heavenly light. Gideon was threshing wheat when God commissioned him, Saul was looking for domestic animals which had strayed from home, Elisha was plowing with twelve yoke of oxen, and Amos was picking the fruit of sycamore trees. None anticipated a heavenly visitation in such unlikely situations.

Do we scorn our lowly stations and our humdrum labors? The arms of heavenly love enfolded the shepherds as they, perhaps in quiet desperation, pursued their daily work with all the wit and courage they could muster. A glory surrounds our most common tasks when we are workmen who are not ashamed of what we do or of the quality of our achievements. Dr. Albert Schweitzer has written, "Plenty of people write to me in hope of getting some spectacular work to do and at the same time they fail to see the worthwhileness of the immediate duty given them." Because of their faithfulness, the shepherds were redeemed from smallness by God who calls no good work mediocre.

Second, to the shepherds of Bethlehem was spoken the most glorious word in the vocabulary of Christmas. That word is "joy." ". . . behold, I bring you good tidings of great joy . . ." (LUKE 2:10)

The New Testament is the most hopeful Book in the world. It reverberates with an exultant, triumphant and victorious joy that surges, permeates and penetrates. The story of creation exhibits "a lip-smacking, exuberant delight in the ingenious beauty and variety of the created world"; the New Testament throbs with such joyous words as these: "Now the God of hope fill you with all joy and peace in believing . . ." (ROMANS 15:13).

If the Bible is the most joyful of all books, Christians should surely be the most joyous of people. Sometimes we are not. Yet the Christian who is a sourpuss has read well neither the signs in the heavens nor the Word of the Lord. Do we too easily resign ourselves to life's buffetings? Resignation is a stoic, not a Christian virtue. Are there frustrations which prayer and fasting do not seem to remove? Are there intolerable situations or, even worse, intolerable persons with whom we are inescapably associated? These a Christian accepts, if he must, and his acceptance is uplifted by a song. For however hard may be the Christian way, both in the traveling and in the attaining of the goal, it is a way of joy. "The Christian is the laughing cavalier of Christ."

This joy is derivative. It is a gift from God in

35

Christ. Our Lord said, "These things have I spoken unto you, that my joy might remain in you, and that your joy might be full" (JOHN 15:11). Genuine joy is a divine legacy. We do not shop for it at the bargain counter in an end-of-the-year clearance sale. Our joy is a confidence born of our trust in God. We are, as Christians, held responsible to "maintain the spiritual glow" (ROMANS 12:11, MOFFATT).

This joy is also reciprocal. Real joy is a contagious thing, something we receive that we may then share it. ". . . such as I have give I thee" (ACTS 3:6).

The word of joy came to the shepherds in the line of duty. And so it comes to us.

Third, after the shepherds had stood in hushed silence before God's revelation in a manger, they did something about it. They became men with a mission. Too often we adore the Baby, and that is all. Nothing happens to us, for nothing happens in us. The wonder of it impels us to—nothing. Not so the shepherds: "And when they had seen it, they made known abroad the saying which was told them concerning this child" (LUKE 2:17). Their joy motivated action. Not only were they the first to be told; they were also the first to tell. In a lively sense, their witness that night made them the first Christian missionaries. These troubadours of God had found something they could not fold carefully in a napkin and bury in a hole.

We come with anticipation to the crib. We must not stop on dead center. Let us go forth to seek and to save. Let us not settle for half a loaf. Sometimes we are pretty miserly about our faith. Real joy always shows, and something ought to rub off in our enthusiasm, in our commitment, in our testimony, and in our desire to share and serve.

An attractive travel brochure, which has come in the mail, invites us to spend Christmas Eve in Bethlehem. That would be wonderful. But if we lack time or money, are we deprived of the shepherds' joy? Not at all, for, if we will, Christmas will come to us.

> Into my heart, into my heart,
> Come into my heart, Lord Jesus;
> Come in today, come in to stay,
> Come into my heart, Lord Jesus.

And if we welcome Him, He will enter, for He stands at our doorstep.

5

A Long Day's Journey Into Light

DOES ANYONE really question whether or not the birth of Jesus is the inexpressibly important event in the history of man? His coming is the great watershed in the chronicle of humanity. We cannot, if we wish, be indifferent to Him. Even our calendars—split between the years before and following His birth—mock our apathy.

But why is His birth of such great consequence? After twenty centuries, why do more than 900 million human beings in every coast and clime honor and reverence Him? By way of suggesting an answer, let us center our thoughts on a poem by one of our distinguished contemporary poets, "Journey of the Magi," by T. S. Eliot. As in all excellent poetry, this poem with verve and clarity probes deeply and lays bare eternal truth.

One of the magi, now old in years and rich in experience, recalls that day long ago when with the others he crossed sand-blown wastelands in pursuit of a beckoning, challenging star:

> *A cold coming we had of it,*
> *Just the worst time of year*
> *For a journey, and such a long journey:*
> *The ways deep and the weather sharp,*
> *The very dead of winter.*

At times during that pilgrimage he remembered the pleasures of the home he had left:

> *The summer palaces on slopes, the terraces,*
> *And the silken girls bringing sherbet.*

And, of course, there were those strangers along the way who taunted him by jeering that his journey was all folly.

> *All this was a long time ago,*

muses the aged magi, who asks,

*Were we led all that way for
Birth or Death?*

He had seen births and deaths before, but

*. . . this Birth was
Hard and bitter agony for us, like Death, our death.*

When he returned once again to his own kingdom, he was a changed man. The old routines and treasured beliefs no longer satisfied him. At Bethlehem all that had died. Something new had been born in him.

The short poem concludes as the old man declares:

I should be glad of another death.

By this he means that he would gladly die again if he might discover anew that kind of spiritual birth.

Such is the substance of Mr. Eliot's poem, but a poem is always more than words and images. It is an impression on the mind, a seed that matures in the imagination, a leaf borne gently on the winds of experience. And this poem suggests far more than it states. It unfolds the true meaning of Christmas. A man of questing faith must give up some things if his life is to be enlarged with new truth, or indeed by Him who is the Truth.

If we come to Christmas burdened with fears and doubts, anxieties and shriveled minds, we shall never know Him who is the Way, the Truth and the Life. These things must go. They must die, if something new—the life and light of God revealed in the Son of His love—is to be born within our hearts.

Jesus said, "Marvel not that I said unto thee, Ye must be born again" (JOHN 3:7). When His life and spirit are born within us, we shall never regret the death of all that we previously may have coveted. Jesus teaches us in words charged with a never-ending pertinence: "Verily, verily, I say unto you, He that heareth my word, and believeth on him that sent me, hath everlasting life, and shall not come into condemnation; but is passed from death unto life" (JOHN 5:24).

To revise slightly, yet significantly, the title of Eugene O'Neill's agonizing autobiographical drama, the magi set out upon a long day's journey into light. And that light may be ours too, if we focus the vision of our hearts upon Bethlehem and Him who is the Light of the world. ". . . if any man be in Christ, he is a new creature: old things are passed away; behold, all things are become new" (II CORINTHIANS 5:17).

6

The Man
Who Missed Christmas

HEROD IS no stranger to the twentieth century. Cut from the same cloth of tyranny as the dictators of our generation, Herod climbed the steppingstones of bribery and butchery to a powerful position that corrupted him and drained from his heart the last lingering vestige of love and compassion. Ultimately, he bequeathed to his people a legacy of bitterness and bloodshed.

Herod became governor of Galilee at the age of twenty-five. He so ingratiated himself with Anthony and Octavius that they appointed him as king. The Roman senate subsequently conferred upon him the title "King of the Jews."

Historical records have distinguished him with the innocuous words of "Herod the Great," for although he was a puppet-ruler and beholden to Roman caprice and whim, he undertook stupendous building enterprises including the building of cities, amphitheaters and pagan temples. His most ambitious plans centered in the building upon Zerubbabel's foundations of the great temple in Jerusalem, a magnificent structure wherein Jesus worshiped. Like many another crafty politician, Herod curried popular favor by offering something to everyone—Roman, Jew and Gentile.

When the Wise Men asked concerning the place where Christ should be born, Herod could not answer. But waving his hand toward Bethlehem, he urged them on their way, saying, "Go and search diligently for the young child; and when ye have found him, bring me word again, that I may come and worship him also" (MATTHEW 2:8).

Of course, Herod had no intention of worshiping the Child. Although he lived in a house of mirrors and feasted on self-adulation, the slightest hint that there might be within his realm a potential rival to his iron-fisted rule brought grave misgivings to his suspicion-tortured mind. Did he dispatch secret agents to dog the steps of the Wise Men? That would have been in character!

Herod shrouded himself in a fog of piety and pretense by saying, ". . . bring me word again, that I may come and worship him also." But even as the silhouettes of the Wise Men faded on the road to Bethlehem, Herod set in motion an ingenious scheme which he believed would forever remove whatever threat to his reign the birth of the Child might portend. He gave orders which brought an unbearable heartache into a multitude of homes: "Then Herod, when he saw that he was mocked of the wise men, was exceeding wroth, and sent forth, and slew all the children that were in Bethlehem, and in all the coasts thereof, from two years old and under, according to the time which he had diligently enquired of the wise men" (MATTHEW 2:16). The Slaughter of the Innocents was a typical Herodian gesture. Had not fear and suspicion long before corroded his mind? When, so he thought, the shadow of intrigue had fallen upon his wife Mariamne, he ordered her execution and that of her two sons by him. The carpet upon which he trod was blood-red with innocent blood.

Men of Herod's stature can brook no opposition. Tyranny always behaves in a similar fashion. In our day we have seen the machinations of dictators who have destroyed all dissenters and exiled or murdered all opponents. No other way is open to them, for they have secured their power by force and they know that always there is the possibility that another force may topple them. ". . . all they that take the sword shall perish with the sword" (MATTHEW 26:52). Nothing is as unstable as a government built only upon might and power.

Down the centuries there have been those who have been afraid of Christ's coming, and those who have known their fondest hopes to be fulfilled in Him. The story of Christianity is a chronicle of those who have rejected and those who have accepted the Son of God.

The birth of the Christ Child did threaten the rule of Herod, but not in the way Herod imagined. Herod believed that the Child would grow into an ardent and persuasive military leader who would link forces with the multitudes of persons who long had suffered under the yoke of despotism. Retributive justice is deeply woven into the fabric of history, and this Herod knew. A few years, and the Child might conceivably become the champion of an irresistible force so potent and powerful that the mercenaries of Herod would be helpless to resist them.

But the Kingdom which Christ's birth promised was not one which the sick mind of Herod could comprehend. To be sure, Christ would rally to His standard millions of discontented peoples, but not for a military struggle nor for armed conflict. Christ's mission was to become a spiritual engagement against the entrenched battalions of wickedness. He would lead but not compel. His would be an army of volunteers whose only weapon would be the power of love.

We who worship the Child have every reason to rejoice with exceeding great joy, for we are citizens of a Kingdom of compassion and salvation. And we even now perceive the foregleams of that day when the kingdoms of the Herods of this world shall become the kingdoms of our Lord, and of His Christ, and He shall reign forever and ever.

Of those persons cast in the drama of the nativity only King Herod did not go to Bethlehem. Herod remained behind and sought diversions to calm his troubled mind. *He was the man who missed Christmas.*

Ironically, he missed what might well have been his golden hour, the privilege of culminating his thirty-three-year reign by laying his crown at the Child's feet. Shortly after the radiant star above Bethlehem faded from sight, death, the inexorable fate of all mortals, brought to an end Herod's life. Knowing that his subjects would rejoice to hear the news of his death, Herod provided that many influential Jews should be executed on the day he died, thereby assuring a general lamentation throughout ham, Isaac, David, the Psalmists, Isaiah, Micah, and many others. God in His own good season would redeem His people through "the anointed one." So it was revealed to Simeon and Anna when the lens of ancient prophecy zeroed in on Bethlehem and the birth of Christ, whose name is the Greek equivalent for the Hebrew word *messiah.*

> *The hopes and fears of all the years*
> *Are met in thee tonight.*

Among the personalities in the nativity story, only Simeon and Anna understood precisely the role in which the Child had been cast. Did the Wise Men comprehend the historical and eternal meaning of Christ's coming? Probably not. Did the shepherds share this insight? Probably not. Could Herod have fathomed the divine purpose of the newborn king? Probably not. But Simeon and Anna knew, and their patient watchfulness and waiting—the vigil of their anxious hearts—were rewarded. Although they surely did not live to witness the completion of Christ's divinely ordained ministry on Calvary, they died in peace, having seen the King who reigns in love and rules by serving, the Deliverer who liberates, and the Saviour who rescues.

Simeon and Anna personify all people, young and

old and of every generation, our own not excluded, whose lives are patterned by great expectations for the redemption, not only of Jerusalem, but of mankind.

The word "redemption" is not in the vocabulary of many present-day Christians, although the word is hallowed by its use in the Bible and in traditional Christian theology. Redemption means to be redeemed, as we might redeem an obligation, or to set free. Man is bound by sin and death. He is helpless to free himself. Only God can release man from his bondage. Simeon and Anna, like their spiritual ancestors, anticipated the day when by God's grace man would be emancipated from his slavery to sin.

The redemption realized through Christ did not come without the payment of a heavy price. Only by being crushed upon the cross could Jesus fulfill the promise of old. The cross can be understood only in terms of the love of God for His sinful children. In His Self-giving on the cross Jesus bore upon Himself the sins of men and reconciled humanity to a heavenly Father from whom they had been estranged by their disobedience.

The angel of the Lord appeared unto Joseph, saying that Mary's child should be called Jesus, "for he shall save his people from their sins" (MATTHEW 1:21). Paul affirmed that "Christ Jesus came into the

"Fear not ye: for I know that ye seek Jesus . . ."
(MATTHEW 28:5).

Even as He was sought after during His ministry in the flesh, so do men today seek to find Him. Where shall we find Him? At this season we are especially reminded that within the whole span of life there is no more important question.

Some wise men of our generation have wondered aloud whether He really can be found. Edwin Arlington Robinson in his poem "Credo" laments:

> *I cannot find my way: there is no star*
> *In all the shrouded heavens anywhere.*

And Archibald MacLeish in *J. B.,* his twentieth-century redaction of the story of Job, bemoans a spiritual climate that hangs heavily over our day:

> *The candles in churches are out.*
> *The lights have gone out in the sky.*

Is there any hope at all that we may find Christ? Will our searching bring us to Him?

Herod missed seeing the Child, but the Wise Men and the shepherds were not disappointed in their quests. There is a chance that we shall miss Him altogether. It could be that we shall become so encumbered in our multitude of Yuletime activities that we shall be exhausted before we get to Bethlehem. Or maybe we shall let others search for Him for us, and await whatever word they may bring back. That is what Herod did, and the Wise Men bypassed him on their journey home. Or our hard hearts may be so flooded with doubt and skepticism that we shall hesitate to believe with our minds what our spirits affirm.

Of this we may be certain: if we fail to find Christ in this season of joyous faith, we shall have little more than a synthetic Christmas. What a tragedy to exchange cards, gifts and greetings, but not to know the radiance of stardust!

To be sure, we shall not now find Him in a crib. He was a Child for only a handful of fleeting years. Nor shall we find Him walking along some hallowed pathway in Palestine. He long since passed from the familiar shores of Galilee. Nor shall we gaze at Him upon a cross or within the dark recesses of a tomb. The cross claimed Him for a narrow day, and the tomb could not bind Him.

Of none other whose name is inscribed upon the annals of history is it said that, having been raised from the dead, He dieth no more. ". . . death hath no more dominion over him" (ROMANS 6:9). The testimony and witness of Christianity is that Christ, though slain by spiritual astigmatism and malignant hate, defied death and rose to everlasting life.

This is a mystery which befuddles our power of explanation and interpretation. Yet, upon this truth, vindicated in the experience of many generations of believers, is established the gospel and the glory of our faith.

And of none other who has shared the garments of mortal flesh is it affirmed that He is a living Personality who may be our constant Companion and ever-living Friend.

By faith Christ lives within our hearts. His spirit is closer to us than our own hands and feet. He has assured us, "I am with you alway . . ." (MATTHEW 28:20). Paul wrote, ". . . I live; yet not I, but Christ liveth in me . . ." (GALATIANS 2:20). ". . . we dwell in him, and he in us . . ." (I JOHN 4:13). Katharine Lee Bates telescopes a vast truth into four brief lines:

> *Not the Christ in the manger,*
> *Not the Christ on the Cross;*
> *But the Christ in the soul,*
> *When all but love is lost.*

This is the supreme and redeeming word which the Christmas message should bring home to each of us: not that we must still seek a Babe in a crib

He outgrew, nor a Teacher who has now moved from the classrooms of Galilee, nor an exhausted Saviour stretched upon a cross, nor a Leader wrapped in the soft linens of death, but rather ". . . Christ in you, the hope of glory" (COLOSSIANS 1:27).